··· A **TIMELINE HISTORY** OF ···

EARLY AMERICAN INDIAN PEOPLES

·· **TIMELINE TRACKERS** : AMERICA'S BEGINNINGS ···

DIANE MARCZELY GIMPEL

Lerner Publications Company
Minneapolis

CONTENTS

Lerner Publications Company
A division of Lerner Publishing Group, Inc.
241 First Avenue North
Minneapolis, MN 55401 USA

For reading levels and more information, look up this title at www.lernerbooks.com.

Library of Congress Cataloging-in-Publication Data

Gimpel, Diane Marczely.
    A timeline history of early American Indian peoples / by Diane Marczely Gimpel.
        pages   cm. — (Timeline trackers: America's beginnings)
    Includes index.
    ISBN 978–1–4677–3638–1 (lib. bdg. : alk. paper)
    ISBN 978–1–4677–4751–6 (eBook)
    1. Indians of North America—History—Chronology. I. Title.
E77.G48 2015
970.004'97—dc23   2013047141

Manufactured in the United States of America
1 – BP – 7/15/14

COVER PHOTO:
The Ute American Indians of western Colorado and eastern Utah created these petroglyphs within what is now Utah's Arches National Park.

INTRODUCTION

When Europeans first came to North America, they called it the New World. But for American Indians, North America was not new at all. Long before European explorers came to the continent, American Indians called it home.

Many historians used to think that the first people arrived in North America about 13,500 years ago. These Asian hunters may have crossed a land bridge that used to link Siberia to Asia. Then they would have continued traveling south. But other clues hint that people lived throughout the American continents much earlier than that—as far back as 20,000 years ago. Since land routes that long ago were blocked by ice, historians think these peoples may have traveled south from Alaska by boat, along the western coast.

However they arrived, these earliest Americans settled throughout the land that eventually became the United States. They belonged to diverse groups, each with its own culture and history. Unlike the Europeans who arrived later, many American Indians did not think of time as having a beginning, a middle, and an end. They understood time as moving in cycles with the seasons and repeating, rather than moving along a straight line. Because of that, American Indians did not look at history as past and would not have plotted it on a timeline like the ones you'll find in this book. Instead, they told the stories of their origins out loud or passed them down through totem poles or by recording them on objects such as rocks or birchbark scrolls. For this reason, many of the timeline events in this book occur after American Indians came into contact with Europeans.

TIMELINES

Timelines are a graphic way of showing a sequence of events over a specific time period. A timeline often reveals the causes and effects of events. It can help to explain how one event in history leads to the next. The timelines in this book show important turning points in the history of some major American Indian groups. Solid lines in the timelines indicate regular intervals of time. Dashed lines represent bigger jumps in time.

CHAPTER 1

The ALASKA NATIVES

Several native groups made their homes in Alaska: the Aleut, the Inuit, the Tlingit, and the Athapascans. These groups are not tribes because members are not part of a single government system. Instead, the

Inuit peoples have traditionally inhabited Alaska, as well as Canada, Greenland, and eastern Siberia.

12,000 BCE: The land bridge connecting Asia and Alaska is covered in water.

20,000 BCE   10,000 BCE   0

Pre-12,000 BCE: The earliest Americans may have crossed a land bridge that then connected Asia to Alaska.

2500 to 1000 BCE: The Aleut and Inuit peoples travel from Asia to North America by boat.

people within each group are often studied together because their cultures are similar and they lived near one another.

Alaskan Natives tended to live near water because it was an important food source. The Aleut lived on a group of islands off the coast of southern Alaska. They shared cultural similarities with the Inuit, who occupied coastal areas. Both groups made kayaks using animal skins stretched over wooden frames. They used them for hunting sea animals, such as seals, otters, walruses, and whales.

Farther south of the Aleut and the Inuit, the Tlingit also settled the Pacific Coast and nearby islands. They fished and hunted sea animals using canoes carved from large trees and hunted land animals using bows and arrows. To their east, the Athapascans moved along rivers. These hunter-gatherers traveled in small groups of family members.

AMERICAN INDIAN CULTURE AREAS

Those who study American Indians often classify native peoples in cultural areas. A cultural area is a region where several different but related groups lived. Scholars choose to do this because the peoples' surroundings determined what food they ate and what weather they faced. Because they would adapt to their surroundings, peoples who lived near one another tended to develop similar cultures.

850–1400 CE:
Some Athapascans from the western subarctic region migrate southward.

500 CE **1000 CE** **1700 CE**

1700s: About 6,000 Inuit, 10,000 Tlingit, 16,000 Aleut, and 13,000 Athapascans live in what is now Alaska.

Different cultures, different houses

Alaskan Natives found many ways to adapt to the harsh climate. The Aleuts lived in large houses with frames made of driftwood and whale bones and walls made of sod. The earthen walls provided insulation from the cold climate. The shelters blended in well with their surroundings.

Like the Aleuts, some of the Inuit lived in partially underground houses made of animal bones and covered in sod blocks. Others had igloos, built using large blocks of ice. People made clothing out of sealskin, which protected against water, and caribou skin, which was warm and lightweight.

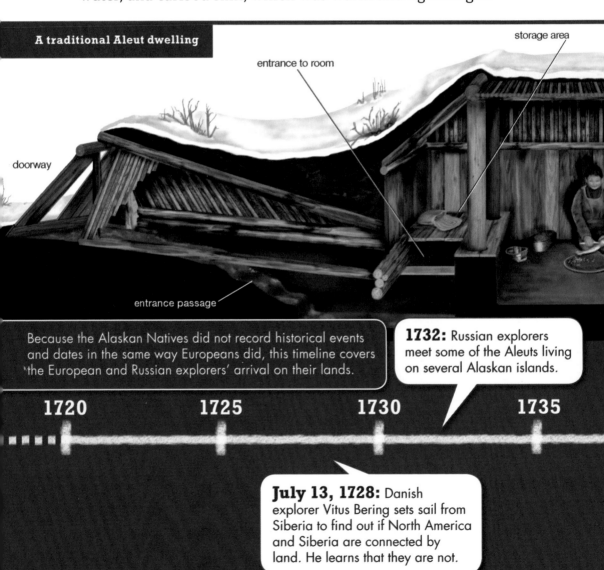

A traditional Aleut dwelling

storage area

entrance to room

doorway

entrance passage

Because the Alaskan Natives did not record historical events and dates in the same way Europeans did, this timeline covers the European and Russian explorers' arrival on their lands.

1732: Russian explorers meet some of the Aleuts living on several Alaskan islands.

1720   1725   1730   1735

July 13, 1728: Danish explorer Vitus Bering sets sail from Siberia to find out if North America and Siberia are connected by land. He learns that they are not.

The Tlingit built large wooden houses. Some houses were big enough to hold fifty people. A village usually had several houses and sheltered a few hundred people each winter. In the summer, the people would go to smaller camps near food sources.

Athapascans had to move around a lot to hunt. They lived in small portable tents made of animal skins and used snowshoes and toboggans to get around in the snow.

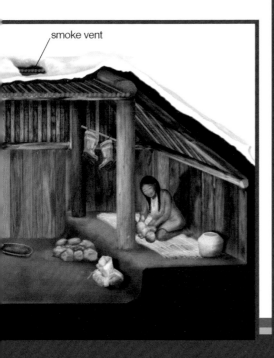
smoke vent

TOTEM POLES

The Tlingit used trees to carve totem poles, either as part of a house or standing alone. All the symbols carved on totem poles had meanings. For example, an eagle meant peace or friendship. A raven meant a hero or a trickster. Together the symbols told stories. Because there was no written language, this was a way that some Alaskan Natives recorded their history.

1740   **1745**   **1750**   **1755**

1741: Bering sees the islands on which the Aleuts live. Tlingit warriors encounter Bering and kill several of Bering's men. Russian explorer Aleksey Chirikov sees the Fairweather Mountain Range in Tlingit territory.

European Contact

The Aleut were among the first Alaska Natives to have contact with Europeans. Russian explorers arrived in the early 1740s. The newcomers made some of the Aleut men their slaves. The Russians took Aleut women and children hostage and forced the men to hunt seals and sea otters so the Russians could sell the valuable animal skins. The Russians brought diseases to which the Aleuts had never been exposed. About 80 percent of the Aleuts died from those diseases within the first forty years after they came in contact with the Russians.

A Tlingit American Indian woman in ceremonial dancing attire

In the late 1700s, the Russians raided Tlingit villages, but the Tlingit fought back. By the end of the century, the Russians had created a settlement in Tlingit territory and

1761: One Aleut group begins to fight back against the Russian invaders by killing an entire party of traders.

1766: The Russians send warships to raid Aleut villages. The Russians destroy the Aleuts' weapons and kill many of their able-bodied men so the Aleuts can no longer wage war.

1760   1765   1770   1775

1762: The Aleut attack and destroy a fleet of five Russian ships.

1778: British explorer James Cook anchors off the coast of Alaska. He is looking for the Northwest Passage—a water route linking the Atlantic Ocean and the Pacific Ocean along North America's northern coast.

founded the Russian-American Company. The Tlingit destroyed the fort and took all the fur pelts. The Tlingit and the Russians continued to fight, and the Russians eventually retreated.

The Inuit of Alaska also first encountered Europeans in the 1740s, but few European fur traders reached their mainland home until the 1800s. Then the Inuit and the Athapascans started trading with the Europeans for weapons and tools.

British explorer Captain James Cook meets American Indians in Alaska.

1784: The first Russian settlement in Alaska is established on Kodiak Island.

1799: Sitka, in Tlingit territory, becomes a European settlement and the capital of Russian America.

1780   1785   1790   1795   1800

1786: French explorer Jean-François de Galaup, comte de La Pérouse, buys an island from the Tlingit and claims it for France.

1800: The Aleut population is about twelve hundred.

CHAPTER 2

NATIVE PEOPLES in the EAST

The Northeast Culture Area

The Northeast Culture Area includes American Indians who settled along the Atlantic coast from modern-day New England to Virginia, as well as in the Ohio Valley, the Great Lakes regions, and parts of modern Canada. They included dozens of groups, such as the Huron, the Iroquois, the Kickapoo, the Ottawa, the Powhatan, the Wampanoag, and the Pequot. While they were spread out over a large area, almost all of these groups spoke one of two types of languages: Algonquian or Iroquoian. Living in

THE IROQUOIS LEAGUE

The Iroquois, who lived in the area of modern New York, included multiple tribes that were allies against attackers. In about 1570, the Cayuga, Mohawk, Oneida, Onondaga, and Seneca peoples formed the League of Five Nations, later known as the Iroquois League. In the early 1700s, the Tuscarora also joined. Other Iroquoian groups, such as the Huron, did not join the league.

1535: French explorers traveling on the St. Lawrence River in New York meet Iroquois people.

1600s: The Iroquois expand their territory to find new sources of fur for trading.

1500   1550   1600

1570: Five Northeast nations establish the Iroquois League. Its constitution is created orally.

woodland areas, they used trees to make their houses, canoes, tools, and weapons. They fished; gathered wild plants; and hunted forest animals including bear, fox, and deer. Some even grew crops such as corn, beans, and squash.

The tribes on the East Coast were among the first to encounter Europeans, who started arriving in the 1400s and the 1500s. In 1535 the Iroquois first met a French explorer who was looking for gold, spices, and sugar. In the 1600s, the French came to trade furs with the Iroquois. The French also introduced new diseases to the area, which killed many American Indians.

The harvest ceremony at the Hopewell burial mound

Early 1700s: The Tuscarora people join the Iroquois League.

| 1650 | 1700 | 1750 |

Mid-1600s: The Iroquois defeat the Huron and other small Iroquoian-speaking tribes, including the Petun, the Neutral, and the Erie. The Iroquois also fight wars against Algonquian-speaking tribes of the Northeast.

Algonquian Peoples Meet White Settlers

In 1607 the English established their first colony, Jamestown, in Powhatan territory. The settlers and the Powhatan, a large group of Algonquian-speaking tribes, fought over land. The marriage of a Powhatan woman named Pocahontas to an English settler briefly helped bring peace in 1613, but fighting soon started again. White settlers wanted more and more land for tobacco crops, and the Powhatan killed hundreds of colonists in an effort to drive them away. The Powhatan eventually were forced onto a reservation.

The Wampanoag, another Algonquian-speaking people in

A Wampanoag home at the Plimoth Plantation historical museum in Massachusetts

1607: The English found their first permanent settlement, Jamestown, in Virginia. The Powhatan capture one of the settlement's leaders, John Smith.

1620: Pilgrims land in Massachusetts and establish the Plymouth Colony.

1600

1610

1620

1613: Powhatan woman Pocahontas marries John Rolfe, bringing temporary peace between the Powhatan and the English settlers.

1621: The Wampanoag sign a peace treaty with the New England Pilgrims. The two groups share a feast that will later become known as the first Thanksgiving.

the Northeast, first had contact with European traders in 1616. The traders unknowingly brought with them a deadly virus, and thousands of the Wampanoag died. When English settlers known as the Pilgrims arrived in 1620, the Wampanoag steered clear of them at first because they feared disease. But eventually the Wampanoag people taught the Pilgrims how to grow corn and where to fish and hunt. According to European accounts, the Wampanoag and the Pilgrims feasted together after the 1621 harvest, a meal that led to the creation of the Thanksgiving holiday.

Massasoit, chief of the Wampanoag people, extends a peace pipe to John Carver, the first governor of the Plymouth Colony, in 1621.

POCAHONTAS

Pocahontas was the daughter of Wahunsonakok, the leader of Powhatan native peoples in Virginia when Jamestown was settled. According to legend, she saved the life of English settler John Smith by preventing her tribe from beheading him. In 1613 the settlers held Pocanhantas hostage in exchange for the release of other prisoners. While in captivity, she met John Rolfe, the man whom she would marry.

1630

1640

1650

1622–1644: English settlers and the Powhatan fight over land rights in the Powhatan War.

1646: The Powhatan sign a peace treaty with English settlers. The treaty sets boundaries for which land belongs to white settlers and which land is reserved for the Powhatan people.

The Pequot War and King Philip's War

Before the 1600s, various Algonquian-speaking peoples had been fighting for control of southern New England. The land there was particularly good for growing crops, and the forests were full of resources. The Pequot were among the most powerful of these groups and came to control most of the land by the early 1600s, when English settlers arrived. The Pequot War broke out in 1636 after the English and Pequot fought over the land. In August 1636, the settlers responded by sending an army to attack and burn American Indian villages.

That winter the Pequot laid siege for months to a settlers' fort in Connecticut. On May 25, 1637, the English forces attacked Pequot chief Sassacus's village, killing more than six

Colonial forces in New England destroy a Pequot village.

Sept. 1636–Apr. 1637: The Pequot lay siege to the English-held Saybrook Fort in Connecticut.

July 1637: Pequot leader Sassacus is captured and executed.

Aug. 5, 1637: The Pequot War ends.

1636   1637   1638

Aug. 24, 1636: Soldiers from the Massachusetts Bay Colony retaliate against the American Indian attacks on English traders by burning a Pequot village on the Pequot River (later called the Thames River) in Connecticut.

May 26, 1637: The English attack a Pequot fort in Connecticut, killing more than six hundred Pequot men, women, and children.

hundred Pequot people. The fighting ended in victory for the English by 1637. Afterward, many surviving Pequot were sold into slavery. In the 1650s, they were freed again and given small pieces of land, although they later lost much of it back to settlers.

By the mid-1600s, the Wampanoag people's relationship with settlers also had soured. The white settlers no longer needed the American Indians' help and had started to take their land. Metacom, called King Philip by the settlers, led a rebellion that began in June 1675 in Massachusetts. By the time the war ended in August 1676, an estimated six hundred Europeans and three thousand American Indians had been killed, including Metacom. The settlers seized even more land, but the Wampanoag survived in some areas.

THE DOCTRINE OF DISCOVERY

When Europeans came to North America, they believed they had the right to take over land occupied by American Indians. Many Europeans based their belief on what was called the doctrine of discovery. The idea came from rulings in the 1400s issued by the pope, the head of the Catholic Church. The pope said Christians could claim land held by non-Christian native people and that these peoples could be converted to Christianity, made into slaves, or killed. While Catholics first voiced this idea, many other Christians came to believe it as well.

June 20, 1675: Wampanoag leader Metacom leads an attack on Swansea, part of the Plymouth Colony in Massachusetts.

June 12, 1676: The English colonists win a battle against 250 American Indians in Massachusetts.

1674

1675

1676

June 28, 1675: The English attack a Wampanoag town near Bristol, Rhode Island.

Aug. 12, 1676: The English colonists kill Metacom, and the Wampanoag-led rebellion ends.

The French and Indian War

While the British were fighting American Indians for land, they also were competing with another group: French settlers. In the mid-1700s, the British and the French began to fight over land in the North American frontier. Many American Indian groups allied with the French because they wanted to push British settlers off their lands. These included Algonquian-speaking tribes in New England and Canada; various American Indians living in the Ohio Valley, such as the Delaware and the Shawnee; the Chippewa; the Ottawa; and some Mohawks in Canada. Some of the Iroquois nations, which considered the Algonquian speakers to be enemies, allied with the British.

British soldiers clash with American Indian warriors near Lake George, New York.

1753: French troops march south from Canada to claim parts of the Ohio Valley. Britain makes a claim to the same area.

July 3, 1754: French and American Indian forces defeat Washington's troops at Fort Necessity in western Pennsylvania.

May 28, 1754: George Washington, a British colonel, leads an attack on a French scouting party near present-day Pittsburgh, Pennsylvania.

May 8, 1756: Britain and France declare war against each other.

1752   1754   1756

Fighting began in 1754, but Great Britain and France did not declare war on each other until 1756. With the help of its American Indian allies, France did well at first. But gradually American Indians gave up the alliance. In 1758 the British promised to stay off the Ohio American Indians' land if they stopped helping the French. The Ohio tribes agreed. Without its allies, the French lost a series of important battles. In 1760 the French lost support of their American Indian allies in Canada and surrendered to the British. That ended the war in North America, although the British and French continued to fight in Europe until 1763.

American Indian allies arrive at a French camp.

Sept. 8, 1760: The French surrender to British forces at Montreal, Canada.

1758   1760   1762   1764

Oct. 21, 1758: The British sign a treaty with American Indian nations, including the Iroquois League and the Ohio Valley American Indians.

Feb. 10, 1763: The French and Indian War, as the conflict is called, ends with the signing of the Treaty of Paris.

The Southeast Culture

In what is now the southeastern United States, many American Indians were not only hunters and gatherers but also farmers. They grew corn, beans, squash, melons, and sweet potatoes. Because of their farming, most groups stayed in one place. These permanent settlements often led to more complex societies. People belonged to different social classes, and leaders inherited their rank. The Southeast American Indians' first contact with Europeans occurred in 1540, when they fought with a group of Spaniards led by Hernando de Soto. In the 1600s and the 1700s, French and British traders made regular visits.

Cherokee chief Cunne-Shote

Among the many peoples that were part of the Southeast Culture Area were the Cherokee people. The Cherokee lived in North Carolina, South Carolina, and Georgia. They lived in houses made of wood and mud that were built around a central council house.

1513: Spanish explorer Juan Ponce de León lands in Florida.

1540: Spanish explorers begin to enter Southeast lands, fighting with American Indians they encounter.

1500

1550

1600

1528: Spaniards claim Florida for Spain.

SOUTHEAST CULTURE

In the French and Indian War, the Cherokee sided with the British. But by the 1760s, the Cherokee had turned against the British. The conflict started after a group of British settlers killed a group of Cherokee men and took their horses. The Cherokee American Indians fought British troops for two years in the Cherokee War. The war ended when British troops burned Cherokee villages and the Cherokee people gave up much of their land.

Three Cherokee American Indian chiefs

1758: The Cherokee side with the British in the French and Indian War.

1650   1700   1750   1800

1673: The French explore the Mississippi River region and find many American Indian groups have been largely destroyed by diseases introduced by the Spaniards.

1760–1762: The Cherokee people fight against the British in the Cherokee War.

CHAPTER 3

NATIVE PEOPLES of the GREAT PLAINS and the GREAT BASIN

The Plains American Indians

The flat and grassy expanse in the middle of the country, stretching from modern-day Texas up to Montana, North Dakota, and Minnesota, is called the Great Plains. Many Plains American Indians grew crops such as corn and beans in fertile river valleys. Because the Plains American Indians tended to stay in one place, they built large permanent houses out of earth.

A Sioux village

1541: Spanish explorers looking for legendary cities of gold find Plains American Indians in Kansas.

850   1500   1550

850: The Plains American Indians begin living in villages. They both hunt and farm.

1500: The Great Plains is mostly occupied by American Indians who farm in fertile river valleys.

In the 1600s, the Spanish brought horses to the Plains area, changing the Plains American Indians' way of life. Being on horseback helped them to hunt buffalo and other large animals. The buffalo provided a source of food, fuel, clothing, and even tools. The Arapaho, the Cheyenne, the Comanche, the Chippewa, the Crow, the Sioux, and others came to depend on hunting more than farming. The Pawnee both hunted and farmed. When the tribes hunted buffalo, they lived in tepees made of buffalo skins. As they moved around more, Plains American Indians developed a sign language to communicate with one another.

Sioux American Indians hunting buffalo

1600s: The Plains American Indians begin using horses to hunt buffalo. Many of them take on a nomadic lifestyle.

1720: A Spanish expedition into the Great Plains is defeated by the Pawnee and Otoe peoples.

1600   1650   1700   1750

1600s–1700s: Several tribes arrive in the Great Plains, including the Arapaho, the Cheyenne, the Crow, the Sioux, and the Chippewa.

Great Basin American Indians

Unlike the Great Plains, the Great Basin is not flat. Its deserts are broken up by mountains, plains, and canyons. The Great Basin Cultural Area includes modern-day Nevada, Utah, Idaho, and parts of Wyoming, Colorado, Arizona, Oregon, and California.

The Great Basin American Indians such as the Bannock, the Paiute, the Shoshone, and the Ute depended mostly on gathering. The main food they gathered was pine nuts. These nuts could be stored easily and then cracked open when needed. The kernels could be ground into flour to make a food called mush. People also had to dig in the ground for roots and insects. Animals were not plentiful in the desert, but sometimes people were able to hunt antelope, rabbits, or other small game. These animals were used for food as well as

A Shoshone hunting party

Because Great Basin American Indians did not record historical information and dates in the same way as Europeans, several of these dates have to do with their contact with Europeans.

1100   1150   1200

1100–1200: The Paiute enter the area of modern-day Utah, Arizona, and Nevada.

for clothing and blankets. Because of the extreme heat and dry land, very few Great Basin American Indians attempted farming.

With meager food supplies, Great Basin tribes moved around a lot in families or small clans. They lived in simple tents with frames made from reeds. In the summer, families went off on their own to hunt and gather, living in temporary structures made of branches.

A drawing by American Indian artist Silver Horn shows an encounter between the Comanche and the Ute.

1300   **1350**   **1550**

1300s: Ancestors of the Western Shoshone and Southern and Northern Paiute enter the Great Basin.

1598: The Spanish settle New Mexico and begin to trade with the Utes.

Great Basin American Indians and Europeans Meet

Great Basin groups first met Europeans in the early 1600s, when Spaniards colonized the area of modern New Mexico. The Ute encountered the Spaniards in the 1630s. At first, relations were peaceful and the groups engaged in trade. The Utes especially wanted the Europeans' horses. Horses allowed the Utes to travel farther and faster. That meant the Utes did not have to move as much, so they began living in larger communities with leaders. The Utes also began hunting buffalo. Later, the Utes started raiding the settlements of other native groups, such as the Paiute, because the Utes wanted more horses. Sometimes the Utes

A European explorer asks directions from an American Indian man.

1604: Spanish explorer Juan de Oñate meets a Paiute while on an expedition.

1649: The Spanish sign a treaty with the Utes. The Spanish start bringing horses into Ute territory.

1600

1650

1700

1638: In New Mexico, the Spanish and the Ute people fight.

abducted Paiute women and children and traded them to the Europeans as slaves.

As in other areas, the Great Basin people suffered from diseases brought in by the Europeans. Europeans also brought livestock into Paiute territory that ate the grasses the Paiute relied on for food.

Leaders from Piegan, Ute, Chiricahua Apache, Comanche, Brule Sioux, and Oglala Sioux tribes gather on horseback.

1776: A Franciscan priest meets the Ute and describes them in his journal as being warlike.

1750   1800   1850

1749: After years of fighting, three Ute leaders make a new peace treaty with the Spanish.

1782: A smallpox epidemic infects the Shoshone, leading them to move into the mountains to recover.

CHAPTER 4

NATIVE PEOPLES of the NORTHWEST

Plateau Peoples

The Plateau American Indians lived in the highlands of present-day Idaho, Montana, and eastern Oregon and Washington. They included the Nez Percé, the Yakama, and other tribes. The Plateau peoples fished in rivers for salmon and other fish. The rivers also provided a way for the native peoples to move around and to trade with other tribes. Other food sources included small game animals, as well as wild berries and other edible plants.

The Nez Percé lived in modern-day Oregon,

A Nez Percé man, wearing a loincloth and moccasins, on horseback

1700   1720   1740

1700s: Native peoples from other culture areas introduce horses to the Plateau region. The Nez Percé grow in power in the Plateau region.

Washington, and Idaho, while the Yakama lived mainly in Washington. In warm weather, members of these groups lived in tents that could be moved easily to follow food sources. In the winter, the Nez Percé took shelter in cone-shaped structures built inside of a pit. The sides were covered in earth and brush for warmth. The Yakama also lived in houses dug into the ground.

After other native peoples brought horses to the Plateau region in the 1700s, the Nez Percé and other Plateau American Indians adapted their culture around the animals. On horseback, the Nez Percé could hunt buffalo and elk. They also trained and bred horses.

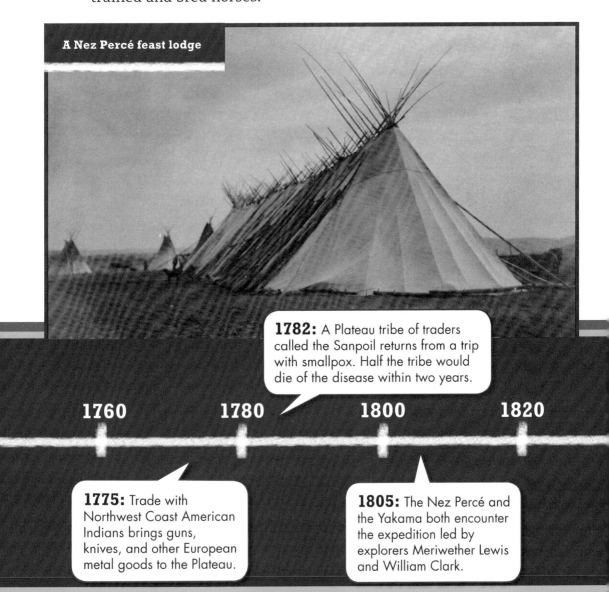

A Nez Percé feast lodge

1782: A Plateau tribe of traders called the Sanpoil returns from a trip with smallpox. Half the tribe would die of the disease within two years.

1760   1780   1800   1820

1775: Trade with Northwest Coast American Indians brings guns, knives, and other European metal goods to the Plateau.

1805: The Nez Percé and the Yakama both encounter the expedition led by explorers Meriwether Lewis and William Clark.

Northwest Coast Peoples

The Northwest Coast culture group thrived along the Pacific coast from Northern California through Oregon and Washington and into Canada. Many of these peoples spoke Chinookan languages and are known collectively as the Chinook. They were whale hunters and fishers. While the Northwest Coast peoples and their Plateau neighbors both included salmon as a major part of their diets, the two culture groups were different in many other ways. People living directly on the coast had plenty of food from the oceans and the forests near their villages, so they did not have to move around as much as the Plateau peoples did to find food.

Many Northwest Coast natives lived in permanent villages of a dozen to forty rectangular houses built of cedar. Each building could house several families.

American Indians spear salmon in the Columbia River.

Because the Northwest Coast peoples did not record historical information and dates in the same way as Europeans, several of the dates on this timeline concern their early contact with Europeans.

1000　　　　　　　**1500**　　　　　　　**1765**

1000: Heavy woodworking tools are in common use along the Northwest Coast.

1500s: Early European explorers reach the coast of modern-day Oregon.

People also used cedar for dugout canoes, totem poles, other carvings, and even clothing. The Chinook built their homes partially underground over pits, in a similar style to that of the Plateau American Indians. Instead of wood carving, they were known for carving sheep horns.

The social structure of Northwest peoples was based on wealth and family. The people with the highest rank would show their status by giving gifts and holding feasts in multiday ceremonies called potlatches.

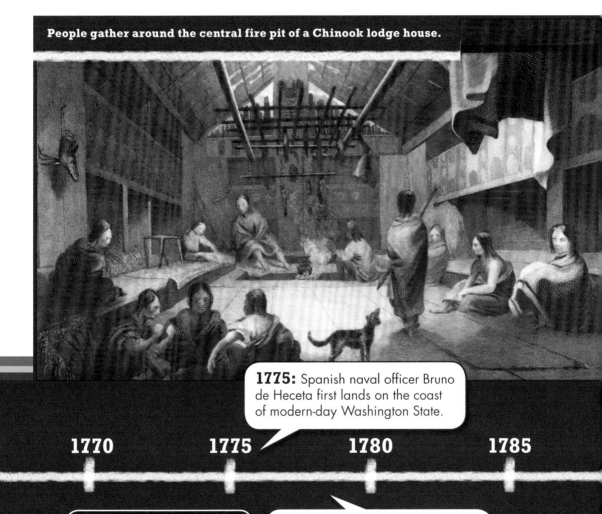

People gather around the central fire pit of a Chinook lodge house.

1775: Spanish naval officer Bruno de Heceta first lands on the coast of modern-day Washington State.

1770   1775   1780   1785

1770s: A smallpox epidemic strikes the Chinook, claiming many lives.

1778: Captain James Cook of the British navy enters the Northwest Coast culture area in a search for the Northwest Passage, a water route across North America to Asia.

Northwest Coast People and Trade

Among the Northwest Coast groups, the Chinook were known for being traders. They traded with other American Indian groups, even those from as far away as the Great Plains. Chinook American Indians traded salmon as well as furs, canoes, shells, and slaves among other tribes. They even had a form of currency made from shells. Traders from different tribes communicated by using a special trading language known as Chinook Jargon. The language was based on a Chinookan language, but tribes all over the Pacific Coast spoke it.

Chinook American Indians used dentalia shells as a form of currency.

1790   1795   1800

1792: Spain establishes the first nonnative settlement in what is now Washington State. British naval officer William Broughton sails the Columbia River and encounters the Chinook people. Trade between Europeans and the Chinook peoples begins.

In 1792 Americans Robert Gray and William Broughton reached the Northwest Territory via the Columbia River. Both British and American trading ships soon followed. Before the end of the 1700s, the Chinook began trading with the British and American merchants.

American Indians paddle canoes to meet a trading ship in the Pacific Northwest.

1805: Explorers Lewis and Clark reach Chinook territory.

1805   1810   1815

1811: An American trading post is established in Chinook territory, and English and French words start to be added to Chinook Jargon.

CHAPTER 5

NATIVE PEOPLES of CALIFORNIA and the SOUTHWEST

The Southwest American Indians

In the southwestern region of what is now the United States, the Pueblo, the Navajo, and the Apache made their homes. The Pueblo included people of different cultures who spoke different

A Pueblo cliff dwelling at Mesa Verde in Colorado

SOUTHWEST AMERICAN INDIANS

500

700

1130

500: The use of bows and arrows makes hunting easier for early Southwest American Indians.

700: The Anasazi, ancestors of the Pueblo American Indians, begin to build multilevel stone dwellings.

700–1130: Success at farming and food storage leads to population growth for native peoples in the Southwest.

languages. The two main groups were the Hopi and the Zuni. They are thought to be descended from the Anasazi and the Mogollon, early inhabitants of the Southwest. The Spanish called all these peoples "Pueblo," the Spanish word for "village." The Pueblo could live in permanent towns because they were successful farmers. They were able to grow corn, squash, and beans in the desert by digging canals to bring water to where it was needed. Their multistory stone dwellings looked like apartment buildings.

The Apache did not have permanent villages but traveled as they hunted buffalo and deer. They were known for raiding other tribes. The Apache lived in wickiups, small, round huts made of earth and twigs. The Navajo lived in cone-shaped houses called hogans, which were made of logs, mud, and tree bark. For a time, they were nomadic hunter-gatherers but later adapted to farming and raising livestock.

Two Navajo hogans in Arizona

1300   1350   1400

Circa 1300: Drought and invasions from other native peoples cause early Southwest natives to abandon their homes and become hunters.

Circa 1400: Some Athapascans have come to the Southwest from the north. They would become the Apache and the Navajo.

The Spanish Enter the Southwest

Spanish explorers entered Pueblo territory in the first half of the 1500s. Soon after the first Spanish explorations, settlers began to arrive. In 1598 Juan de Oñate brought 129 colonists to found the colony of New Mexico. The newcomers taught the Southwest American Indians how to grow new crops, but they also forced them to pay taxes and obey Spanish laws. The Acoma Pueblo people tried to fight off the Spanish but lost. Many became slaves. Afterward, other Pueblo American Indians cooperated with the Spanish.

Spanish Jesuit missionaries try to convert American Indians to Christianity.

1500s: Apache bands begin raiding Spanish settlements.

1450

1500

1550

1539: Spanish explorer Marcos de Niza reaches Zuni territory.

In 1680 the Pueblo fought back again, in what was called the Pueblo Rebellion. The Spanish had been punishing Pueblos for practicing native religions. On August 11, 1680, a Pueblo named Popé, leading American Indians from multiple villages, attacked Spanish soldiers and priests. Popé's rebels were able to force the Spanish out of New Mexico. But the Spaniards returned in 1692 and ruled the area until the 1800s.

The Spanish also encountered other Southwest peoples in the 1500s and the 1600s, including the Apache and the Navajo. The Spanish tried to convert these natives to Christianity but had little success. The Apache and later the Navajo fought back by raiding Spanish settlements. The Apache and Navajo took cattle and horses from the settlers. Later, they took people to turn them into slaves.

Spaniards and American Indians fighting

1598: The Spanish create their first settlement in Pueblo territory and establish a North American capital in the area of what is now Sante Fe, New Mexico.

1692: The Spanish regain control of the Pueblo.

1600   **1650**   **1700**

1593–1630: Diseases brought by the Spanish devastate Southwest peoples.

1600s: The Spanish first meet the Navajo.

1680: The Pueblo people revolt against the Spanish and force the Spanish out of New Mexico.

California American Indians

Some of the practices of Southwest cultures could be found in the neighboring California culture area to the west. In fact, California natives incorporated elements of all the neighboring cultural areas prior to European contact. For example, American Indians in northwestern California used the trees there to build rectangular houses and to make dugout canoes, much as the American Indians in the Northwest Coastal area did. Because California is big and varied, many different native cultures existed there. Most coexisted peacefully.

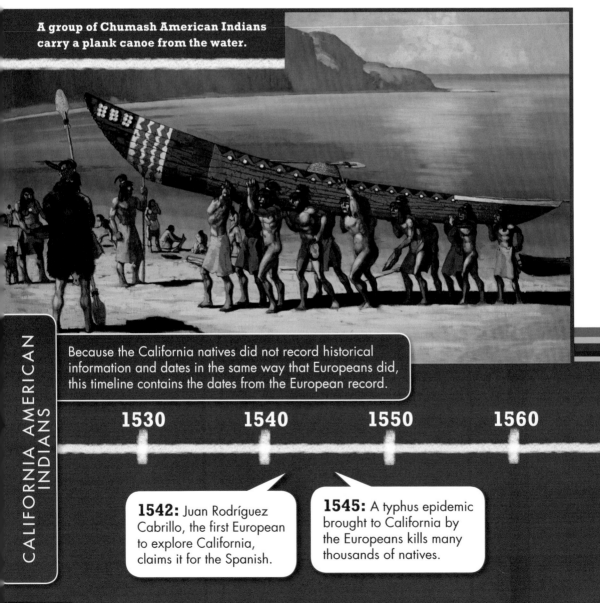

A group of Chumash American Indians carry a plank canoe from the water.

Because the California natives did not record historical information and dates in the same way that Europeans did, this timeline contains the dates from the European record.

1530　　**1540**　　**1550**　　**1560**

1542: Juan Rodríguez Cabrillo, the first European to explore California, claims it for the Spanish.

1545: A typhus epidemic brought to California by the Europeans kills many thousands of natives.

In general, California tribes did not farm much. Instead, they hunted, fished, and gathered edible plants. The Chumash tied together planks to make boats for fishing and traveling. They lived in cone-shaped houses built of branches in central California and on islands off the coast.

Farther inland, Pomo American Indians and other groups gathered acorns to survive. Women would take the kernels out of the acorns, dry them in the sun, and pound them into flour. They would pour boiling water over the flour to remove a bitter acid from it. They used the flour to make soup, mush, or bread. They also ate fish and hunted for small game animals.

Chumash homes in California

1579: Sir Francis Drake arrives in California and claims the land for England.

1570   1580   1590   1600

1500s: California is home to about 133,000 American Indians before European explorers arrive.

1602: A Spanish merchant named Sebastián Vizcaíno explores the southern part of California and names the port of San Diego.

Influence of Spanish Missionaries

The first Europeans to come to California were the Spanish, who arrived in the first half of the 1500s. However, the Spanish did not try to establish a colony in California for another two hundred years.

Change came to the people of California in 1772 with the arrival of Spanish missionaries. The missionaries eventually built twenty-one missions along the coast. They wanted to convert the California American Indians to Christianity and force them to farm. Instead, the Spanish missionaries made thousands of American Indians into slaves. American Indians were forced to give up their ways of life to work on the farms that supplied the missions. Those who did not cooperate were treated harshly or even killed. In 1775

SPIRITUAL DIFFERENCES

Although the American Indian nations had different traditions and beliefs, most of them believed that all things had souls, or spirits. This included not just people but also animals, plants, rocks, and weather. From the American Indian point of view, all of these things depended on one another and were equal. This differed from the Europeans' point of view. Most Europeans believed only humans had souls and ranked above the rest of the living and nonliving things in the world, which existed to be used by the people.

1772: The Spanish begin to build missions in California and to enslave the California natives.

1760   1770   1780   1790

1769: Father Junípero Serra, a Spanish missionary, leads an army up the California coast and founds a mission at San Diego.

1775: A group of California natives tries to revolt against the Spanish but is unsuccessful.

a group of American Indians tried to revolt. They burned down one of the Spanish missions. But Spanish soldiers quickly put an end to their rebellion.

Thousands of American Indians who died of abuse or European diseases were put in mass graves. The surviving American Indians remained enslaved. The California American Indians were not released from slavery until the 1800s.

The Mission San Diego de Alcala prior to the 1775 revolt

1800   1810   1820   1830

1834: After gaining independence from Spain, the Mexican government frees American Indian slaves in California.

Conclusion

The area that is now the United States was a diverse and complex place prior to the arrival of Europeans in the 1400s. The vast land with so many different climates and such widely varied landscapes led those native to the area to develop different ways of living. They all had a long history in North America prior to the continent's settlement by outsiders.

American Indians were also all forever changed by their encounters with European newcomers. They were introduced to horses, European weapons, and different cultural practices. Their populations were reduced by conflict and disease. In addition, their resources were depleted by the influx of settlers.

In the 1600s, Europeans began placing American Indians on reservations. In the 1830s, the forced removal of southeast American Indians from their lands became known as the Trail of Tears. By the middle of the 1800s, the US government made American Indian removal an official policy. The government often used treaties to purchase large amounts of land from American Indians and promised to provide things such as education and health care in return. Many of the promises made by the government were later broken.

The hardships American Indians faced after Europeans came to their land had a significant impact on their ways of life. A large number of American Indians on reservations lost their

May 28, 1830: The US Congress approves the Indian Removal Act. It offers American Indians unsettled western prairie land in exchange for giving up land east of the Mississippi River.

1825   1850   1875

1830s: Southeastern American Indians are forced to relocate to land west of the Mississippi River. Thousand die during the trek, known as the Trail of Tears.

1862: The US Congress passes the Homestead Act, which encourages settlement by Americans in the Midwest, Great Plains, and the West.

right to self-govern. They lost touch with their religious practices when such practices were outlawed. And young American Indians, who were often forced to attend government schools, were made to speak only English in the classroom.

Yet in spite of the cultural losses they endured, American Indian groups survived and even thrived through the years. They established their own governments and worked to revive their cultural traditions. They also fought for economic security and recognition of their unique political status as nations.

Older generations of American Indians have handed down their sense of independence as peoples to younger generations. They have also passed along their traditions. Their efforts help ensure that these societies will live on for many years to come.

Government buildings such as this one in Window Rock, Arizona, are a common sight on reservations. Many American Indian groups have established governments to manage their own communities.

1932: Under the Dawes Act, white settlers acquire two-thirds of the land previously reserved for American Indians.

1900   1925   1950   1975

1887: The Dawes General Allotment Act gives pieces of land to individual American Indians. It encourages American Indians to become farmers by promising them a chance to gain US citizenship. Land not given to individuals for farming is sold publicly.

1960s: The civil rights movement, which focuses on winning equal rights for people of all races, leads to activism on behalf of American Indian groups.

Writing Activity

Imagine that you are a member of one of the American Indian groups in this book and that you are encountering Europeans for the first time. You could be a Pueblo American Indian meeting the Spanish missionaries in California or a Wampanoag helping the Plymouth Pilgrims through their first winter, for example.

First, write about this experience from an American Indian person's perspective.

What do you think about the Europeans?

How do you hope they will treat you?

How does your life change after they arrive?

Imagine the same events from a European person's perspective.

How do you react to meeting the American Indians?

How do you treat them?

How do you plan to settle disputes over land and resources?

Glossary

ally: to join or offer support

culture: the beliefs, customs, and practices of a group

missionary: a person who goes to a foreign land to do religious work

nomadic: moving from place to place rather than having a single home

orally: spoken instead of written

plateau: an area of high, level ground

reservation: an area of land set aside for people of a particular culture to live on

settlement: a place where people set up a community

territory: an area of land under the control of a ruler or a group

LERNER

SOURCE™

Expand learning beyond the printed book. Download free, complementary educational resources for this book from our website, www.lernerresource.com.

Further Information

Annenberg Learner Interactives—United States History Map
http://www.learner.org/interactives/historymap/indians2.html
This site from Annenberg Learner offers brief histories of American Indian groups from the different culture areas of the United States.

Gibson, Karen Bush. *Native American History for Kids*. Chicago: Chicago Review Press, 2010. Find out more about the early history of America's native peoples and about famous American Indians.

Gondosch, Linda. *Where Did Sacagawea Join the Corps of Discovery? And Other Questions about the Lewis and Clark Expedition*. Minneapolis: Lerner Publications, 2011. Learn about Meriwether Lewis and William Clark's encounters with American Indians as they ventured through America's Northwest.

History: Native American Cultures
http://www.history.com/topics/native-american-history/native-american-cultures
This site, from A&E Television Networks, provides information about many historical topics, including the cultures of American Indians.

Josephson, Judith Pinkerton. *Why Did Cherokees Move West? And Other Questions about the Trail of Tears*. Minneapolis: Lerner Publications, 2011. Find out more about how the US government moved American Indians to American Indian Territory in Oklahoma.

MacFarlan, Allan. *Native American Tales and Legends*. Mineola, NY: Dover Publications, 2001. Read myths, tales, and other stories from various American Indian groups.

Native American Facts for Kids
http://www.native-languages.org/kids.htm
Visit this website to find information about a number of topics related to American Indians: their history, their culture, and their lives today.

Index

Photo Acknowledgments

The images in this book are used with the permission of:© Werner Forman /Universal Images Group/Getty Images, p. 5; © Universal History Archive/The Bridgeman Art Library, p. 6; © Universal Images Group Limited/Alamy, p. 8; © Danita Delimont/Gallo Images/Getty Images, p. 9; The Granger Collection, New York, pp. 10, 16; © The Stapleton Collection/The Bridgeman Art Library, pp. 11, 25; © Langdon Kihn/National Geographic Society/CORBIS, p. 13; © Prisma Archivo/Alamy, 14; © Peter Newark Pictures/The Bridgeman Art Library, p. 21; © North Wind Picture Archives/Alamy, pp. 15, 18, 26, 30, 33, 41; © Ivy Close Images/Alamy, p. 19; © Peter Newark American Pictures /The Bridgeman Art Library, pp. 20, 36 © Peter Newark Western Americana /The Bridgeman Art Library, pp. 22, 23 © INTERFOTO/Alamy, p. 24; © Everett Collection Historical/Alamy, p. 27; Library of Congress, pp. 28, 29; © MPI /Getty Images, p. 31; © Dave Marsden/Alamy, p. 32; © Robert Wyatt/Alamy, p. 34; © David South/Alamy, p. 35; © Look and Learn/The Bridgeman Art Library, p. 37; © National Geographic Images/Alamy, p. 38; © Marilyn Angel Wynn/Nativestock/Getty Images, p. 39; AP Photo/Felicia Fonesca, p. 43.

Front Cover: © iStockphoto.com/fotoMonkee.

Main text font set in Caecilia Com 55 Rom 11/16.
Typeface provided by Linotype AG.